Dear Parent:
Your child's love of reading starts here!

Every child learns to read in a different way and at his or her own speed. Some go back and forth between reading levels and read favorite books again and again. Others read through each level in order. You can help your young reader improve and become more confident by encouraging his or her own interests and abilities. From books your child reads with you to the first books he or she reads alone, there are I Can Read Books for every stage of reading:

SHARED READING
Basic language, word repetition, and whimsical illustrations, ideal for sharing with your emergent reader

BEGINNING READING
Short sentences, familiar words, and simple concepts for children eager to read on their own

READING WITH HELP
Engaging stories, longer sentences, and language play for developing readers

READING ALONE
Complex plots, challenging vocabulary, and high-interest topics for the independent reader

I Can Read Books have introduced children to the joy of reading since 1957. Featuring award-winning authors and illustrators and a fabulous cast of beloved characters, I Can Read Books set the standard for beginning readers.

A lifetime of discovery begins with the magical words "I Can Read!"

Visit www.icanread.com for information on enriching your child's reading experience.

Visit www.zonderkidz.com/icanread for more faith-based I Can Read! titles from Zonderkidz.

"My God sent his angel. And his angel shut the mouths of the lions. They haven't hurt me at all."
—*Daniel 6:22*

ZONDERKIDZ

The Beginner's Bible Daniel and the Lions' Den
Copyright © 2008 by Zondervan
Illustrations © 2017 by Zondervan

An **I Can Read Book**

Requests for information should be addressed to:

Zonderkidz, 3900 Sparks Dr. SE, Grand Rapids, Michigan 49546

ISBN 978-0-310-76041-2 (softcover)

Ilusrator: Denis Alonso
Art Direction: Jody Langley

Printed in China

22 23 24 25 /DSC/ 8 7 6 5

ZONDER**kidz**   SHARED My First READING   **I Can Read!**

Daniel and the Lions' Den

Daniel was a good man.

He loved God very much.

The king loved Daniel.

Daniel helped the king.

Because he loved God, some men
did not like Daniel.

The men made an evil plan.

The men went to the king.

"King, you are a great man,"

they said.

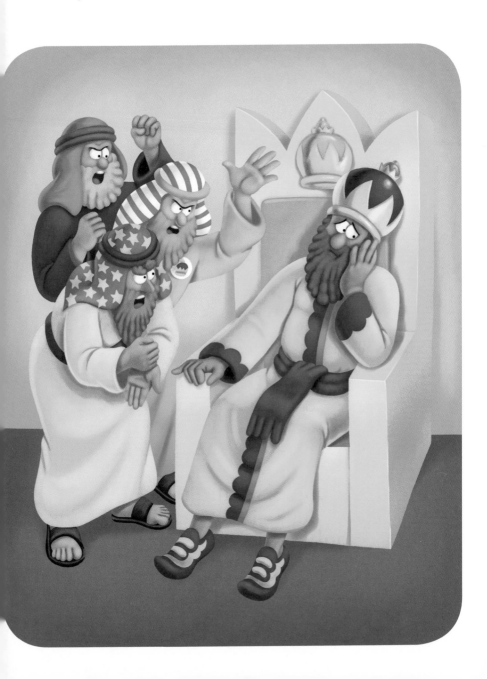

"People should pray

only to you."

The men said, "If they do not,
we will put them
in the lions' den."

The men wanted to get Daniel
in big trouble.

The king said, "Okay."

He did not know it was

a trap for Daniel.

Daniel prayed only to God.

The men saw Daniel praying.

He did not stop praying to God.

The men told the king

about Daniel.

"King, your helper Daniel
does not obey your rule,"
the men said.

"Daniel was praying

to God. Not to you."

The men had tricked the king.

Guards came to take
Daniel away to the
lions' den.

The king shook his head.

The rule said pray

only to the king.

But Daniel would not stop.

He would pray only to God.

The king did not
want to hurt Daniel.

The king said, "Daniel, I hope your God will save you."

Daniel was thrown into
the lions' den.
The king was very sad.

Daniel prayed to God.

He asked God to watch

over him.

So God sent his angel

to help Daniel.

Daniel was safe all night.

In the morning,

the king woke up.

He ran to see Daniel.

The king called, "Daniel,

are you okay?

Did your God save you?"

"Yes," said Daniel.

"God's angel helped me

with the lions!"

The king was so happy!

"Come with me, Daniel."

The king told all his people,

"Daniel's God is great!

Let us pray only to God."